Boosting Aussie Kids' Vocabulary

© C. R. Draper 2015

All rights reserved. No part of this book may be reproduced or transmitted in any form or by any means without written permission of the author.

Published: achieve2day, 2015

ISBN: 978-1-909986-10-7

Contents

1. Big and small 7
2. Male and female relationships 8
3. Animal babies 9
4. Where we live 10
5. –ice and –ise 11
6. Feathers and fins 12
7. Measuring 13
8. Synonyms, antonyms and homophones 14
9. Idioms 15
10. To, too, two 16
11. Words with more than one meaning 17
12. Difficult spellings 18
13. Fast and slow 19
14. 'i' before 'e' except after 'c' 20
15. One, two, three 21
16. We're, wear, where and ware 22
17. Instrument families 23
18. Idioms 24
19. Word endings 25
20. Strong and weak synonyms 26

21. Difficult spellings 27
22. Synonyms 28
23. Old and new 29
24. Idioms 30
25. Male and female 31
26. Body parts 32
27. Difficult spellings 33
28. Antonyms 34
29. Homophones 35
30. Religions 36
31. Adding -ing and -ed 37
32. Meat 40
33. Idioms 41
34. Difficult spellings 42
35. Synonyms 43
36. Antonyms 44
37. Trees and flowers 45
38. Words ending in -ance and -ence 46
39. Idioms 48
40. Homophones 49
41. 'Shun' suffixes 50
42. Synonyms 52

43. Antonyms 53
44. it's, its and who's, whose 54
45. Countries – Asia and South America 55
46. Homographs 56
47. Difficult spellings 57
48. Plurals – words ending in o and y. 58
49. Idioms 59
50. Synonyms 60
51. Antonyms 61
52. Homophones 62
53. Countries - Europe and Africa 63
54. Difficult spellings 64
55. Homographs 65
56. Idioms 66
57. Colours 67
58. Synonyms 68
59. Antonyms 69
60. Sport 70
61. There, they're and their 71
62. Homophones 72
63. Homographs 73
64. Idioms 74

65. Difficult spellings 75
66. Collective nouns (animals) 76
67. Synonyms 77
68. Antonyms 78
69. Prefixes 79
70. Homographs 81
71. Idioms 82
72. Friend and foe 83
73. -ight and -ite 84
74. Plurals – f and v 85
75. Homophones 86
76. Difficult spellings 87
77. Synonyms 88
78. Antonyms 89
79. Becoming a verb 90
80. To be or not to be 91
81. Outer space 92
82. Homophones 93
83. Homographs 94
84. Plurals 95
85. Idioms 96
86. Antonyms 97

87.	Comparatives and superlatives	98
88.	Difficult spellings	99
89.	Collective nouns (not animals)	100
90.	Idioms	101
91.	Shopping	102
92.	Capital cities - Europe	103
93.	In the garden	104
94.	Idioms	105
95.	Synonyms	106
96.	Antonyms	107
97.	Capital cities – non-European	108
98.	Homophones	109
99.	Homographs	110
100.	Onomatopoeia	111
Answers		112

1. Big and small

Put the following words into the correct column below:

Word bank:

large, huge, enormous, tiny, average, colossal, medium, microscopic, gargantuan, infinitesimal, miniature, gigantic, mammoth, minute, little, massive, monstrous, miniscule, intermediate, humongous, moderate, small

---

Small	Medium	Big

2. Male and female relationships

Match the words below:

> Word bank:
>
> mother, son, uncle, niece, brother, daughter, sister, father, husband, grandmother, grandfather, nephew, wife, aunt

Male	Female
brother	_____
_____	niece
_____	mother
uncle	_____
husband	_____
_____	grandmother
son	_____

3. Animal babies

Match the babies with the animals:

> Word bank:
>
> calf, calf, calf, puppy, foal, foal, kitten, kitten, lamb, cub, pup, fawn, kid, piglet

Animal	Baby
cat	
cow	
deer	
dog	
dolphin	
elephant	
giraffe	
goat	
horse	
lion	
pig	
rabbit	
sheep	
zebra	

4. Where we live

List the following from smallest to largest:

> Word bank:
>
> city, hamlet, country, village, town, county, continent

_____
_____
_____
_____
_____
_____
_____

Write a definition for the word hamlet:

_____
_____
_____

5. –ice and –ise

If it is a verb: -ise
If it is a noun: - ice
I can advise (verb) you to take my advice (noun), which is to practise (verb) your English practice (noun). This rule only applies in the very few cases where both word forms exist.

Choose the correct version in the sentences below:

1. Kareena needed to (practice, practise) the piano.
2. William Wilberforce helped bring the (practice, practise) of slavery to an end in Britain.
3. I would (advice, advise) you to listen to your parents.
4. Heed my (advice, advise) as it will help you get into a grammar school.
5. My (advice, advise) is that you do a lot of (practice, practise) papers before your exam.
6. Joseph wanted to (device, devise) an electronic (device, devise) that would help him (practice, practise) his maths.

6. Feathers and fins

Classify the following animals as birds or fish:

> Word bank:
> heron, sole, cod, kiwi, grebe, teal, trout, herring, grouse, quail, salmon, bass, petrel, carp, cormorant, whiting, flounder, bittern, ibis, spoonbill, perch, hake, plaice, kite, tit, bream, eel, buzzard, coot, tern, mackerel, guppy

Birds	Fish

7. Measuring

Match the types of measurements and their units using the words below.

Word bank:

gram, litre, second, degree Celsius, metre cubed, mile per hour, capacity, metre, minute, kilometre per hour.

	Units	
mass	_____	
length	_____	
volume	1. _____	2. _____
speed	1. _____	2. _____
time	1. _____	2. _____
temperature	_____	

What is another word for volume? _____

8. Synonyms, antonyms and homophones

Synonyms are words which have the same or similar meaning.

Antonyms are words with the opposite meaning.

Homophones are words that sound the same but have a different meaning.

> Wordbank:
>
> left, fix, brake, write, damage, correct.

From the word bank find:

A synonym for right - _____
An antonym for right - _____
A homophone for right - _____

A synonym for break - _____
An antonym for break - _____
A homophone for break - _____

9. Idioms

Match the saying with the meaning:

Sayings:
1. A stitch in time saves nine.
2. Too many cooks spoil the broth.
3. Just toe the line.
4. In hot water.
5. He said it tongue in cheek.
6. Bite your tongue

Meanings:
A. If too many people are involved in a task, the quality of the task may suffer.
B. Just do what you are told / supposed to do.
C. Stop yourself from talking.
D. In trouble.
E. He was joking.
F. Fixing something sooner stops it becoming more damaged and harder to fix.

Answers:
1. _____, 2._____, 3._____, 4._____, 5._____, 6._____,

10. To, too, two

'To' involves direction.

'Too' means also or too much (more than enough)

'Two' is the number 2.

Write the correct version (to, too or two) in the sentences below.

Josh was going _____ take _____ children _____ the beach. "It is _____ hot _____ go today," said Josh.

"That's a pity," said Katerina, "I wanted to go _____."

"OK," said Josh, "maybe we can go in _____ days time."

"I hope so," said Marsha.

"I hope so _____," said Josh.

11. Words with more than one meaning

Many words have more than one meaning. For example kind can mean a type of thing or to be caring

>eg. A Labrador is a kind of dog.
>She was kind and caring.

In the sentences below find a word that can be put in both spaces.

1. I would _____ a burger with _____.
2. The room was very _____ and airy, but the desk in the corner was heavy, not _____.
3. The _____ was a meeting with some of the main world leaders and was held not far from the _____ of the mountain.
4. She told me in _____ that he reason she didn't perform in the concert was because she lacked _____.
5. I think we will _____ to our original plan and _____ the poster on the wall of how to roast a marshmallow on a _____.

12. Difficult spellings

> Word bank:
> occasion, separate, enough, ache, cough, bought, fourth, height, acceptable, cemetery

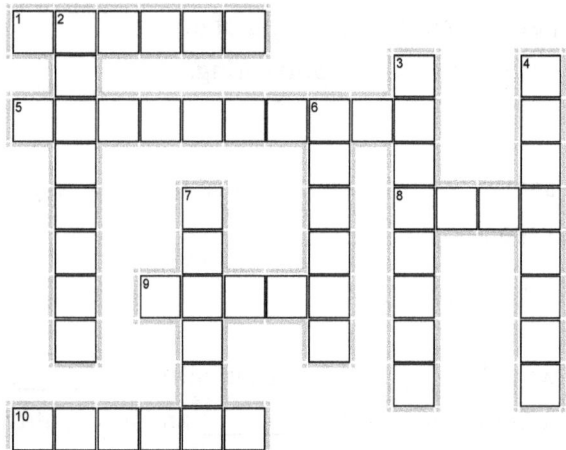

Across

1. He came _____ in the race.
5. It is not _____ to lie or cheat.
8. After the run, he had an _____ in his side.
9. When she had a cold, the _____ was very annoying.
10. You had to be over a certain _____ to go on the ride.

Down

2. She bought a new dress, as meeting the Queen was a special _____.
3. For the recipe you need to _____ the egg white from the yolk.
4. The funeral was held in the _____.
6. She _____ some apples at the shops.
7. I have had _____ to eat, thank you.

13. Fast and slow

Put the following words in the correct column below.

> Word bank:
>
> speedily, meandering, slowly, leisurely, quickly, swift, promptly, frantic, sluggish, rapid, sedate, crawl, plodding, hastily, hurriedly, dawdling

Fast	Slow

14. 'i' before 'e' except after 'c'

The saying:
> *'i' before 'e' except after 'c,'*
> *But only when it rhymes with 'e.'*

can help with many words such as brief and receive. Unfortunately there are many exceptions such as protein, weird, seize, weigh, weight, heir and either.

Write 'ie' or 'ei' in the spaces below.

1. Do not dec_ _ ve me, I want the truth.

2. He was so tall he could touch the c _ _ ling

3. He rec _ _ ved the award with humility.

4. He paid the cash _ _ r before leaving.

5. He was rel _ _ ved to know he had passed.

6. The scientists found a new spec _ _ s of animal.

7. They won because the other team forf _ _ ted.

8. The w _ _ ght of the parcel increased the postage.

9. They carefully excavated the anc _ _ nt ruins.

10. It is w _ _ rd that a plane has gone missing.

15. One, two, three

Fill in the corresponding words below:

1	2	3
one		
once		
single		
first		

Mono and uni mean one. Bi and di mean two. Tri means three. Write the correct prefix (mono, uni, bi, di or tri) in the spaces below.

1. A _____cycle has two wheels, a _____cycle has three but a _____cycle has only one.
2. Something that is _____chrome contains only one colour.
3. Someone who can speak two languages fluently is _____lingual.
4. A conversation between two people is a _____alogue, but it felt like a _____logue because he kept talking and I couldn't get a work in edgeways.

16. We're, wear, where and ware

"We're" is a contraction of "we are".
"Wear" is to wear clothes or to destroy by friction or use. Also can mean to tolerate or accept.
"Where" is asking in what direction, place or position.
"Ware" refers to things for sale or items of a particular type.

Write the correct word in the sentences below.

1. What should I _____ to the party?
2. That is _____ I need to go.
3. The market stalls had lots of lovely china _____.
4. _____ going to Cornwall this afternoon.
5. Acid rain will make the rock _____ away faster.
6. That's _____ it is, I've been looking for that.
7. The crystal _____ was very beautiful.
8. Hurry up, _____ hungry!
9. Can you find _____ Kenya is on this map?
10. Excessive _____ and tear made the bicycle unusable.

17. Instrument families

Put the instruments in their correct family

Word bank:

violin, cornet, trumpet, bassoon, piccolo, viola, double bass, trombone, French horn, cello, flute, guitar, sitar, banjo, tuba, harp, clarinet, recorder, bugle, lute, saxophone, oboe

String	Woodwind	Brass

18. Idioms

Match the saying with the meaning:

Sayings:
1. A bird in the hand is worth two in the bush.
2. You can't have your cake and eat it too.
3. Kill two birds with one stone.
4. To sit on the fence.
5. Add insult to injury.
6. A piece of cake.

Meanings:
A. You can't have is both ways. Sometimes you have to choose between two desirable alternatives.
B. To make a negative situation worse.
C. A task that is easy.
D. To accomplish two different things at the same time.
E. It is better to have something that is certain than the possibility of more.
F. To not want to choose or make a decision.

Answers:
1. _____, 2. _____, 3. _____, 4. _____, 5. _____, 6. _____,

19. Word endings

Generally:

- words ending in –le are nouns or verbs
- words ending in –el or –il are nouns
- words ending in –al are nouns or adjectives.

So principle is a noun meaning a general rule or idea. Principal is normally an adjective meaning main or most important. However, principal can also be a noun referring to someone who is the most important person in an organisation or performance.

Complete the missing letters in the sentences below.

1. The princip _ _ violinist was very famous.
2. I will not lie, on princip _ _.
3. There is amp _ _ room for all of us.
4. They loved the rur _ _ countryside.
5. She put lots of bas _ _ in the spaghetti sauce.
6. To get all the water in, why not use a funn _ _ ?
7. Please do not start _ _ me.
8. Please stick the lab _ _ on your book.
9. The tid _ _ waves were very large.

20. Strong and weak synonyms

Some synonyms have a stronger or weaker meaning.

For example, damp means a little bit wet, while saturated means completely soaked (really wet.)

Number the synonyms below, weakest first:

1. angry, furious, annoyed
2. freezing, cool, cold
3. good, great, excellent
4. happy, content, ecstatic
5. depressed, sad, melancholy
6. hard, awkward, difficult
7. small, tiny, miniscule
8. nice, enchanting, alright
9. cheap, expensive, affordable
10. ravenous, peckish, hungry
11. soggy, moist, saturated

21 Difficult spellings.

One word in each sentence below is misspelled.
Underline the word and write it out correctly:

1. He was embarased when his mum kissed him goodbye. _____

2. The firey furnace was very hot. _____

3. The forein students visited the school for a week. _____

4. The existance of aliens is debated. _____

5. Do not exede the speed limit. _____

6. The computer came with a three year garantee. _____

7. You should get along and not harrass each other. _____

8. When pigs are mixed they fight to establish a hiarachry, based on weight. _____

9. Ignarence, or not knowing is no excuse. _____

10. The fuel gage was very low. _____

22. Synonyms

Choose the synonym of the words below:

Word bank:

amaze, commence, bias, clever, chuckle, always, damp, mimic, part, tip, stubborn, frugal

	Synonym
intelligent	
fraction	
start	
point	
prejudice	
thrifty	
forever	
moist	
copy	
obstinate	
surprise	
giggle	

23. Old and new

Put the following words in the correct column below:

> Word bank:
>
> modern, recent, ancient, antique, present, stale, fresh, previous, current, past, contemporary, aged

Old	New

24. Idioms

Match the saying with the meaning:

Sayings:
1. He has a chip on his shoulder.
2. Break a leg.
3. He can't cut the mustard.
4. You're driving me up the wall.
5. To bend over backwards
6. To keep your chin up.

Meanings:
A. Not of a good enough standard.
B. Prepared to make an effort; willing to do whatever it takes.
C. To remain positive in a difficult situation.
D. Good luck.
E. Upset or angry about something that happened in the past.
F. You are really annoying me.

Answers:
1. ____, 2. ____, 3. ____, 4. ____, 5. ____, 6. ____,

25. Male and female

Match the male and female word:

Word bank:

Queen, duke, host, princess, duchess, count, countess, steward, stewardess, heir, heroine, actor, heiress, hero, actress, King, prince, hostess

Male	Female

26. Body parts

Underline the internal (inside) organs.

head, arm, lung, liver, leg, knee, brain, stomach, wrist, ankle, intestine, heart, finger, thumb, shoulder, kidney, hip, neck, elbow, foot, pancreas, toe, knuckles, ear, skin

Complete the analogies below:
Elbow is to arm as _____ is to leg.
Ankle is to leg as _____ is to arm.

From the words above, choose the correct body part.
1. Pumps blood around the body. _____
2. Filters blood producing urine. _____
3. In the middle of your fingers. _____
4. Where oxygen enters your body. _____
5. Used to hear. _____
6. An upper limb. _____
7. Food is absorbed. _____
8. Contains lots and lots of nerve cells. _____

27. Difficult spellings

One word in each sentence below is misspelled.
Underline the word and write it out correctly.

1. It is bizzarr how some words are spelled. _____

2. Your colleege, is a person that you work with. _____

3. The comittee will make a decision. _____

4. It is definately Tuesday today. _____

5. I'm not sure how to solve this dilemna. _____

6. He was in ekstesy, when he won. _____

7. She looks really familliar to me. _____

8. He is a really good freind. _____

9. The story was very humorus. _____

10. Come here, imedietely. _____

11. He had a party, when he turned fourty.

    _____

12. It was complex, but he got the general jist.

    _____

28. Antonyms

Make an antonym for the following words by adding the correct prefix. The first one has been done for you.

The possible prefixes are: dis, in, il, im, un, non.

	Antonym
happy	unhappy
tidy	
obedient	
usually	
polite	
logical	
action	
sense	
flexible	
legal	
appropriate	
pure	
available	
complete	
agree	

29. Homophones

Choose the correct word in the sentences below:

1. Can I have a (peace, piece) of cake please?
2. Careful, it is (quite, quiet) difficult.
3. They were hungry and the table was (bare, bear).
4. They enjoyed the (leak, leek) and potato soup.
5. He was very pleased to (meat, meet) the Queen.
6. It took him the (hole, whole) week to dig the (hole, whole) in the garden.
7. The woodpecker (board, bored) a hole in the tree.
8. She felt very (weak, week), for a (weak, week) after the operation.
9. He wondered (aloud, allowed) why he was not (aloud, allowed) to talk in class.
10. Can you please (poor, pour) me a glass of juice.

30. Religions

Complete the table for each of the religions below:

> **Word bank:**
>
> Jew, Sikh, Church, Temple, Christian, Hindu, Muslim, Synagogue, Mosque, Gurdwara

Religion	Person	Place of Worship
Christianity		
Hinduism		
Islam		
Judaism		
Sikhism		

31. Adding -ing and -ed

When adding –ing or –ed to words here are a few rules you need to keep in mind:

- If the verb ends with a 'silent e', then drop the final -e.
  eg. Bake becomes baked or baking.

- A few verbs keep the final -e when adding -ing to distinguish them from similar words. For example, singe becomes singeing rather than singing.

- Verbs ending in -ee, -ye, and -oe (such as free, dye, and tiptoe) do not drop the final e.
  eg. Dye becomes dyed or dyeing.

- Verbs that end with a single vowel plus a consonant, and the stress is at the end of the word, double the final consonant.
  eg. Stop becomes stopped or stopping but open becomes opened or opening (stress not on the last syllable).

- Verbs that end with a vowel plus -l, double the l.
  eg. Equal becomes equalled or equalling.

More rules for adding –ing or –ed to words.

- Verbs that end with two vowels and a consonant, generally the final letter is not doubled.
  eg. Seal becomed sealed or sealing.

- Words that end in –ie, change the ie to y when adding –ing but not when adding –ed.
  eg. Die becomes died or dying and
  tie becomes tied or tying.

- Word that end with –y, which forms a syllable, change the y to i when adding –ed but not when adding –ing.
  eg. Carry becomes carried or carrying.

- Verbs that end with -c, add a -k
  eg. Mimic becomes mimicked or mimicking.

- Most other words don't change.
  eg. Play becomes played or playing.

Unfortunately, as with most rules in English there are exceptions; such as handicap becomes handicapped.

Add – ed and –ing to the following words:

Word	Add -ed	Add -ing
talk	talked	talking
hunt		
cry		
bore		
surprise		
lie		
study		
ski		
plan		
exit		
answer		
cancel		
group		
repair		
bar		
occur		
stir		
pour		
admit		
target		
traffic		

32. Meat

Match the types of meat below to the animals they come from:

Word bank:

Beef, lamb, mutton, veal, venison, pork, bacon / ham

Animal	Meat
young cow	_____
older cow	_____
deer	_____
pig	_____
pig (preserved)	_____
young sheep	_____
older sheep	_____

33. Idioms

Match the saying with the meaning:

Sayings:
1. To find your feet.
2. To cry wolf.
3. Once in a blue moon.
4. A drop in the ocean.
5. A dime a dozen.
6. To have butterflies in the stomach.

Meanings:
A. Anxious or nervous, especially when anticipating something.
B. Common, easy to get.
C. Occasionally.
D. To intentionally raise a false alarm.
E. To become confident in the situation.
F. A small, normally insignificant, part of something much bigger.

Answers:
1. _____, 2. _____, 3. _____, 4. _____, 5. _____, 6. _____,

34. Difficult spellings

Choose the correct spelling in the following sentences:

1. The fire (completly, completely) destroyed the building.
2. I am (concious, conscious) that it is late.
3. Filled with (curiosity, curiousity) she looked through the window.
4. How did all the cake (disapear, disappear) so quickly?
5. Her face was very (familar, familiar).
6. It (happend, happened) very quickly.
7. She wanted to be (independant, independent).
8. Please do not (interrupt, interupt) me.
9. There is so much (knowlege, knowledge) to learn.
10. It is (neccessary, necessary) to wear sunscreen.
11. Is the repair (noticable, noticeable)?
12. Clearly, this is not an everyday (occurance, occurrence).
13. Can you please (separate, seperate) the blocks.
14. The party was a big (suprise, surprise).
15. He speaks (truely, truly) about what happened.

35. Synonyms

Choose the synonym of the words below:

Word bank:

absurd, abrupt, endorse, agree, erect, shame, respect, persuade, juvenile, impede, calm, brief

	Synonym
concur	
concise	
coax	
honour	
sudden	
immature	
pacify	
hinder	
humiliate	
upright	
ludicrous	
support	

36. Antonyms

Choose the antonym of the words below:

> Word bank:
>
> order, flippant, calm, contract, wild, eccentric, natural, hidden, pessimist, plentiful, wild, aware, grave

	Antonym
conventional	
chaos	
artificial	
optimist	
serious	
oblivious	
meagre	
tense	
captivity	
expand	
obvious	
trivial	

37. Trees and flowers

Circle the words below that are trees.

Underline the words which are not circled and are a type of flower.

beach, beech, daffodil, elm, lily, daisy, petunia, pansy, larch, fuchsia, oak, carnation, ceremony, startle, tulip, rhododendron, conifer, yew, violet, mauve, pine, satin, mahogany, buttercup, bluebell, willow, livery, geranium, poplar, hazel, cornflower, tartan, hyacinth, maple, iris, platinum, orchid, birch, honeysuckle, primrose

38. Words ending in -ance and -ence

Some of these words you just need to know.
However, here are a few rules to help.

- If the word is from a verb that ends in -y, -ure, or -ear, then the ending will be -ance.
  e.g. endure becomes endurance.

- If the main part of the word ends in a 'hard' c or a 'hard' g, then the ending will be spelled -ance. e.g. significance.

- If it is related to a verb ending in -ate, then the ending is normally –ance.
  e.g. dominate becomes dominance.

- If the word is from a verb ending in -ere, then the ending will be spelled -ence.
  e.g. adhere becomes adherence.
  The word perseverance is an exception.

- If the main part of the word ends in a 'soft' c or a 'soft' g, then the ending will be spelled -ence. e.g. innocence.
  The word vengeance is an exception.

Make these into words ending in -ance or –ence:

absent	_____
allow	_____
annoy	_____
appear	_____
coherent	_____
confident	_____
conscious	_____
different	_____
diligent	_____
elegant	_____
grieve	_____
guide	_____
ignore	_____
instant	_____
patient	_____
persist	_____
relevant	_____
resist	_____

39. Idioms

Match the saying with the meaning:

Sayings:
1. Don't put all your eggs in one basket.
2. Don't count your chickens before they are hatched.
3. Cross that bridge when you come to it.
4. Burn the midnight oil.
5. On the ball.
6. A slap on the wrist.

Meanings:
A. Do not put all your resources in one possibility.
B. To work late into the night.
C. Do not plan anything that depends on a good thing you hope to happen in the future.
D. Mild punishment.
E. Deal with a problem if and when it becomes necessary, not before.
F. To know and understand the situation well.

Answers:
1. _____, 2. _____, 3. _____, 4. _____, 5. _____, 6. _____,

40. Homophones

Choose the correct word from the word bank.

> Word bank:
> vain, vein, vane, tail, tale, sum, some, cereal, serial, hair, hare, blew, blue

1. Fine thread-like strands growing from the skin of an animal. _____
2. A type of mammal. _____
3. A story. _____
4. Found on the rear part of some animals. _____
5. A story or play appearing in regular instalments. _____
6. Eaten for breakfast. _____
7. A colour. _____
8. Past tense of "to blow." _____
9. To add up. _____
10. A few of something. _____
11. A broad blade pushed by the wind. _____
12. Blood vessel that returns blood to the heart. _____
13. Having an excessively high opinion of oneself. _____

41. 'Shun' suffixes

When adding suffixes that make the sound 'shun' you may need to change the ending of the word first.
eg. collide becomes collision.

The suffixes that make the sound 'shun' are:

- 'tion' eg educate becomes education.
- 'ssion' eg discuss becomes discussion.
- 'cian' eg music becomes musician.
- 'sion' eg explode becomes explosion.

The ending of the root word, generally indicates what the ending should be.

The word should end in 'tion' if:

- The root word ends in –ate
- The root word ends in any consonant other than –d, –n, -l or –r.

The word should end in 'sion' if:

- The root word ends in –l or –d.
- The root word ends in –de, se, -ss or –mit,

Root word	Word with suffix added
act	*action*
complete	
confuse	
connect	
demonstrate	
devote	
direct	
distribute	
electric	
emit	
extend	
optic	
permit	
persuade	
possess	
promote	
provide	
reduce	
replicate	
success	

42. Synonyms

Choose the synonym of the words below:

> Word bank:
>
> consent, offender, excessive, tumble, soil, spoil, curt, guess, scoop, dismal, greedy, grow

	Synonym
fall	
blunt	
agree	
gluttonous	
cultivate	
ruin	
culprit	
gloomy	
dirty	
shovel	
lavish	
estimate	

43. Antonyms

Choose the antonym of the words below:

Word bank:

arrogant,, real, lethargic, reckless, turbulent, dishevelled, debilitate, forget, fragile, after, cumbersome, virtuous

	Antonym
humble	
cautious	
alert	
easy	
robust	
corrupt	
still	
feigned	
recall	
neat	
preceding	
strengthen	

44. it's, its and who's, whose

It's is a contraction of it is or it was. Its is the possessive. Just remember "It's an apostrophe."

Similarly, who's is a contraction of who is or who has. Whose is the possessive of who.

Underline the correct word in the sentences below:

1. (Who's, Whose) watching TV?
2. (Who's, Whose) book is this?
3. (It's, Its) a very hot day.
4. Do you think (it's, its) very easy to do?
5. England has changed (it's, its) attitude towards drinking tea.
6. (Who's, Whose) side are you on?
7. (Who's, Whose) in the kitchen?
8. (It's, Its) time to go.
9. The snake had shed (it's, its) skin.
10. (It's, Its) 800m around the track.

45. Countries – Asia and South America

Put the countries below in the correct continent.

Japan, Mexico, Peru, China, Malaysia, Singapore, Argentina, Brazil, India, Pakistan, Colombia, Thailand, Cambodia, Ecuador, Korea, Chile, Mongolia, Brunei, Bolivia, Guyana, Myanmar, Laos, Paraguay, Venezuela, Nepal, Vietnam, Uraguay

Asia	South America

46. Homographs

Which word has both of the meanings below:

> Word bank:
> coordinates, chest, wind, minute, invalid, fan, well, lean, present, date

1. Movement of air.
   Present tense of wound. _____
2. A shaft sunk into the ground to obtain water, oil or gas.
   Not sick. _____
3. The points on a graph or map.
   Goes well with other pieces. _____
4. Weak or disabled.
   Not legally acceptable. _____
5. A supporter.
   Something that creates movement of air for cooling. _____
6. Meat with little fat.
   Be in a sloping position. _____
7. A gift.
   Now. _____
8. Tiny.
   A unit of time. _____
9. A type of storage container.
   The front of a person's body between the neck and the diaphragm. _____
10. A day in the month.
    Dark brown oval fruit. _____

47. Difficult spellings

Underline the correct spelling, in each line below.

1. acommodate, accomodate, <u>accommodate</u>
2. forseable, forseeable, <u>foreseeable</u>
3. <u>glamorous</u>, glamourous, glamorus
4. aincent, <u>ancient</u>, anceint
5. rythem, rhithem, <u>rhythm</u>
6. <u>sieve</u>, seive, sive
7. superceed, <u>supersede</u>, supercede
8. acidently, <u>accidentally</u>, accidentaly
9. ocurrence, occurence, <u>occurrence</u>
10. hite, <u>height</u>, hieght
11. <u>acquire</u>, aquire, achoir
12. columme, <u>column</u>, columm
13. libary, <u>library</u>, libarie
14. manetinance, maintanence, <u>maintenance</u>
15. miniture, minature, <u>miniature</u>
16. <u>memento</u>, meminto, momento
17. goverment, <u>government</u>, governmint
18. happend, hapened, <u>happened</u>
19. independant, <u>independent</u>, indapendent
20. interupt, <u>interrupt</u>, interuped

48. Plurals – words ending in o and y.

To make some words into plurals we just add an 's.' In words ending with 'o,' sometimes 'es' is added and sometimes just 's.' For example: potato becomes potatoes but piano becomes pianos.

Write the plural of the words below:

1. solo   _____
2. zoo   _____
3. tomato   _____
4. hero   _____
5. radio   _____
6. logo   _____
7. echo   _____
8. buffalo   _____
9. mosquito   _____
10. zero   _____
11. mango   _____
12. taco   _____

If a word ends in a 'y' we change the 'y' to an 'i' and add 'es.'

13. library   _____
14. berry   _____
15. activity   _____

49. Idioms

Match the saying with the meaning:

Sayings:
1. Adding fuel to the fire.
2. All Greek to me.
3. All bark and no bite.
4. At the drop of a hat.
5. Back to the drawing board.
6. Beating around the bush.

Meanings:
A. Unable to be understood.
B. Have to start over again.
C. Doing or saying something to make a bad situation worse.
D. Avoiding talking about the main topic.
E. Will do something immediately.
F. Speech makes them appear scarier than actions would suggest.

Answers:
1. _____, 2._____, 3._____, 4._____, 5._____, 6._____,

50. Synonyms

Choose the synonym of the words below:

Word bank:

stingy, eager, continue, neutral, bountiful, flexible, safe, answer, remorse, retreat, spontaneous, confident

	Synonym
proceed	
supple	
miserly	
solution	
impromptu	
keen	
withdraw	
assured	
secure	
regret	
generous	
impartial	

51. Antonyms

Choose the antonym of the words below:

Word bank:

clear, advance, trivial, common, friendly, competent, ample, fake, serious, generous, ignore, fail

	Antonym
recognise	
hostile	
important	
real	
accomplish	
miserly	
rare	
frivolous	
opaque	
scarce	
recede	
inept	

52. Homophones

Underline the correct word in the sentences below:

1. He (guessed, guest) that the (guessed, guest) was about 40 years old.
2. He (war, wore) clothes that had been repaired many times during the (war, wore) due to war rations.
3. His (boarder, border) came from just near the (boarder, border) of Belgium and France.
4. He needed the (receipt, reseat) for the work the repairman had done to (receipt, reseat) the tap washer.
5. The (made, maid) had (made, maid) the beds by ten o'clock.
6. The rafting had really (wet, whet) his appetite for more, even though he became very (wet, whet).
7. He (threw, through) the ball (threw, through) the hoop.
8. If you get bitten by a (might, mite), you (might, mite) feel a little unwell.
9. He decided to (seas, seize) the opportunity to go sailing on the (seas, seize).
10. He walked to the end of the (peer, pier), to (peer, pier) into the distance.

53. Countries - Europe and Africa

Put the countries below in the correct continent.

France, Belgium, Tanzania, Botswana, Tunisia, Ghana, Chad, Spain, Hungary, Turkey, Kenya, Greece, Ireland, Austria, Swaziland, Poland, Lichtenstein, Zimbabwe, Nigeria, Cameroon, Guinea, Ukraine, Germany, DR Congo, Denmark, Madagascar, England

Europe	Africa

54. Difficult spellings

Choose the correct spelling in the following sentences.
1. She was a very (intellagent, inteligent, intelligent) young lady.
2. The (graffitti, graffiti, grafitti) was hard to remove.
3. The lion was very (fierce, fierse, fearse).
4. The early Egyptians wrote on (papyrus, papyrous, pappirus).
5. (Diseduous, Decidous, Deciduous) trees lose their leaves in Autumn.
6. Keep going (untill, un-till, until) you reach the end.
7. The (twelth, twelfth, twelveth) day of Christmas is the day before Epiphany.
8. The homework (scedoole, scedule, schedule) was demanding.
9. He made the announcement (publickaly, publicly, publicaly).
10. He had already filled in the (questionaire, questionnaire, questionair).
11. The teacher wasn't sure of the (pronounciation, pronounceation, pronunciation) of the name.
12. Writing computer games was his (pasttime, pasthyme, pastime).

55. Homographs

Which word has both of the meanings below:

> Word bank:
> duck, swallow, bat, down, refuse, foot, bow, pupil, close, band

1. A unit of length.
   Part of the body. _____
2. Cause something to go down the throat.
   A type of migratory bird. _____
3. Near.
   To shut. _____
4. A group of musicians.
   A flat, thin strip of material. _____
5. A weapon for shooting arrows.
   To bend the head or upper body as a
   sign of respect. _____
6. To lower the body to avoid a blow.
   A type of bird. _____
7. Rubbish.
   To not accept. _____
8. Student.
   Part of the eye. _____
9. A mammal.
   Used to hit a ball. _____
10. At a lower level.
    Soft, fine fluffy feathers. _____

56. Idioms

Match the saying with the meaning:

Sayings:
1. Put a sock in it.
2. A scapegoat.
3. Water under the bridge.
4. Every cloud has a silver lining.
5. Jump on the bandwagon.
6. To see eye to eye.

Meanings:
A. Something that is in the past and no longer important.
B. Even in very negative situations, there is something positive.
C. Someone who takes the blame for the mistakes of others.
D. Be quiet.
E. To agree on something.
F. Join a popular trend or activity.

Answers:
1. _____, 2. _____, 3. _____, 4. _____, 5. _____, 6. _____,

57. Colours

Put the colours in the correct column below:

> Word bank:
>
> blue, violet, cerise, lemon, burgundy, aqua, peach, apricot, mauve, rouge, gold, crimson, cyan, purple, scarlet, amber, cream, maroon, indigo, azure, turquoise

Red	Purple	Yellow / Orange	Blue / Green

58. Synonyms

Choose the synonym of the words below:

Word bank:

amend, glitch, pristine, reliable, suggestion, ardour, implement, zealous, prevail, aperture, consequence, manage

	Synonym
unspoilt	
bug	
apply	
dominate	
effect	
passion	
dependable	
handle	
avid	
opening	
correct	
hint	

59. Antonyms

Choose the antonym of the words below:

> Word bank:
>
> hidden, merry, unrelated, wicked, jeer, useful, hide, pleasant, thaw, simple, ample, lose

	Antonym
grave	
discover	
complicated	
pious	
praise	
meagre	
exposed	
triumph	
odious	
futile	
pertinent	
freeze	

60. Sport

Underline the team sports (sports *always* played as a team). Circle the indoor board games.

volleyball, softball, scrabble, bridge, lacrosse, hockey, cycling, tennis, dressage, rowing, football, netball, chess, rounders, basketball, gymnastics, swimming, athletics, javelin, diving, tae-kwon do, backgammon, triathlon, bocce, badminton

Which sport (from those listed above)?
1. Uses cards. _____
2. Uses a shuttlecock. _____
3. Is a type of horse riding. _____
4. Is done at a swimming pool but is not swimming. _____
5. Involves making words on a board. _____
6. The bishop moves diagonally. _____
7. Can be done in a velodrome. _____
8. Consists of swimming, cycling and running. _____

61. There, they're and their

There refers to a place – over there.
They're is a contraction of they are.
Their is the possessive pronoun meaning belonging to them.

Underline the correct form in the sentences below:

1. What does the sign over (their, there, they're) say?
2. They just rang to say that (their, there, they're) running late.
3. I've met them before but I've forgotten (their, there, they're) names.
4. I don't think (their, there, they're) happy.
5. I enjoyed visiting on holidays but wouldn't want to live (their, there, they're).
6. I need to go to (their, there, they're) concert.
7. Is (their, there, they're) any dessert left?
8. (Their, There, They're) growing up fast.
9. This is (their, there, they're) 25th wedding anniversary.
10. I think (their, there, they're) coming to join us.

62. Homophones

Underline the correct word in the sentences below:

1. He put the iron (oar, **ore**) into the boat and then used the (**oars**, ores) to pull away from the shore.
2. This (thyme, **time**) the cook added some (**thyme**, time) for flavouring.
3. When he accidentally hit his (**humerus**, humorous) bone, he didn't find it very (humerus, **humorous**).
4. The caterer turned the (earn, **urn**) on to make the teas and coffees, This helped them (**earn**, urn) their good reputation.
5. The (root, **route**) the hikers took meant they had to climb over a large tree (**root**, route).
6. The thief could not (**steal**, steel) the large (steal, **steel**) ornament as it was too heavy.
7. The eagle was too (soar, **sore**) to (**soar**, sore) above the clouds.
8. I (**heard**, herd) that there is a buffalo (heard, **herd**) near here.
9. He ate some (**currants**, currents) while trying to measure the electrical (currant, **current**).
10. The medicine came in a small (**vial**, vile) and tasted really (vial, **vile**).

63. Homographs

Which word has both of the meanings below:

> Word bank:
> ball, fine, colon, rock, sink, clear, bass, gum, evening, incense

Which word has both of the meanings below:
1. To move back and forth.
   A stone _____
2. To remove people or objects.
   Transparent. _____
3. To make smooth.
   The latter part of the day. _____
4. A spherical object.
   A type of dance. _____
5. A sticky substance secreted by some trees.
   To clog up. _____
6. To fall or drop gradually to a lower level.
   A drain or sewer. _____
7. Of excellent quality.
   A sum of money imposed as a penalty._____
8. To make angry.
   Perfume or fragrance. _____
9. Low in pitch.
   A type of fish. _____
10. Part of the large intestine.
    A punctuation mark. _____

64. Idioms

Match the saying with the meaning:

Sayings:
1. Like a chicken with its head cut off.
2. Get off on the wrong foot.
3. Over my dead body.
4. Over the top.
5. To kick the bucket.
6. On the same page.

Meanings:
A. Will absolutely not allow that to happen.
B. To agree on something.
C. Making a bad start to a relationship or task.
D. Die.
E. Rushing around fast, all over the place.
F. Very excessive.

Answers:
1. ____, 2. ____, 3. ____, 4. ____, 5. ____, 6. ____,

65. Difficult spellings

One word in each sentence below is misspelled. Underline the word and write it out correctly:

1. He needed a fishing <u>lisense</u> for the camping trip. _____ license
2. The <u>existance</u> of aliens is possible. _____ existence
3. The haunted house was <u>eirie</u>. _____ eerie
4. They built a large <u>extention</u> on their house. _____ extension
5. She walked <u>accross</u> the road. _____ across
6. He painted with both watercolour and <u>acryllic</u> paint. _____ acrylic
7. There was an <u>abundent</u> supply of water. _____ abundant
8. I <u>loath</u> to see her upset. _____ loathe
9. They worked hard to <u>mantain</u> the high standards. _____ maintain
10. You should <u>obay</u> your parents. _____ obey
11. We can now <u>procede</u> with the plan. _____ proceed
12. Is the information <u>relevent</u>? _____ relevant

66. Collective nouns (animals)

Match the collective noun with the animals:

Word bank:
army, caravan, colony, dray, flock, flock, flutter, herd, murder, pack, parliament, pod, pride, school, swarm, tower

Animal	Collective noun
ant	_____
bat	_____
bee / wasp	_____
bird	_____
buffalo	_____
butterfly	_____
camel	_____
crow	_____
dog	_____
dolphin	_____
fish	_____
giraffe	_____
lion	_____
owl	_____
sheep	_____
squirrel	_____

67. Synonyms

Choose the synonym of the words below:

Word bank:

abominable, conspicuous, forsake, detrimental, precarious, abhor, acknowledge, vanish, feeble, method, decompose, impromptu

	Synonym
spontaneous	
unstable	
disappear	
abandon	
approach	
detest	
detestable	
weak	
admit	
obvious	
decay	
harmful	

68. Antonyms

Choose the antonym of the words below:

Word bank:

refuse, dusk, flow, dawdle, lazy, knowledge, scarce, reveal, waste, guest, tenant, voluntary

	Antonym
abundant	
hasten	
industrious	
economise	
accept	
host	
landlord	
ebb	
conceal	
ignorance	
dawn	
compulsory	

69. Prefixes

Prefixes are groups of letters added to the beginning of words which can change the words meaning. Some common prefixes, and their meanings, include:

- ad – to, towards
- af – tending towards
- al – all
- a – in or on
- ante – before
- anti – against
- extra – beyond
- in – into or not, without
- inter – between
- out – more than others or separate
- over – too much
- pre – before
- pro – for
- post – after, later
- semi – half or partly
- under – below, beneath

Choose the correct prefix:

1. To stick to something else: _____fix
2. A liquid which when added to water lowers the freezing point: _____freeze
3. Describes a noun: _____jective
4. The time leading up to Christmas: _____vent
5. A room forming an entrance to another room: _____room.
6. Someone who has lots of money: _____fluent
7. Baby born early: _____mature
8. On fire: _____blaze.
9. Before a particular time: _____date
10. One of the best in the field: _____standing
11. To recommend or inform: _____vise
12. After school, not part of the main school curriculum: _____curricular
13. Between countries: _____national
14. To put off until a later date: _____pone
15. Clouds covering the sun: _____cast
16. The arrival of a large number of people or things: _____flux
17. Stop something happening: _____vent
18. Throw with the hand below the waist: _____arm
19. Not fully awake: _____conscious
20. Creating or controlling a situation rather than just responding to it: _____active

70. Homographs

In the sentences below find a word that can be put in both spaces.

> Word bank:
> desert, lead, leaves, produce, park, present, row, patient, can, shed

1. He _____ the party.
   The _____ on the tree have turned brown.
2. The dog _____ a lot of hair, so was made to sleep in the _____.
3. The local _____ with a playground now has a convenient car _____.
4. He was asked to _____ an expedition down the _____ mine.
5. They had a _____ while in the _____ boat causing it to capsize.
6. Once I _____ the fruit, I _____ sell them at the local market.
7. The manager was asked to _____ a special _____ to an employee for his service to the company.
8. The gardener aimed to _____ the best _____ at the local market.
9. The soldier chose to _____ his unit while in the _____.
10. The _____ had to be very _____ while waiting for the doctor to discharge him.

71. Idioms

Match the saying with the meaning:

Sayings:
1. The bee's knees.
2. Costs an arm and a leg.
3. A hot potato.
4. The icing on the cake.
5. Hear it on the grapevine.
6. Blood is thicker than water.

Meanings:
A. The best.
B. A controversial issue.
C. To hear something as rumour or gossip.
D. Family ties are very strong.
E. Expensive.
F. Something very good, on top of an already good situation.

Answers:
1._____, 2._____, 3._____, 4._____, 5._____, 6._____,

72. Friend and foe

Put the words in the word bank into the correct column below:

Word bank:
friend, foe, enemy, companion, ally, supporter, opponent, rival, comrade, associate, adversary, competitor, combatant, mate

Friend	Foe

73. -ight and -ite

Finish the words with either "ight" or "ite."

1. It was a very br_____ light.
2. She enjoyed flying her k_____.
3. He enjoyed the helicopter fl_____.
4. Please wr_____ a letter.
5. The science encyclopaedia will really exc_____ his curiosity.
6. The pl_____ of the relatives was heartbreaking.
7. You must be pol_____ at all times.
8. This lid is on very t_____.
9. It is now n_____, so I'm going to bed.
10. Turn left and then the next road r_____.
11. The musicians wore black trousers with a wh_____ shirt.
12. This m_____ help with your dilemma.
13. A m_____ is not an insect as it has eight legs.
14. Finishing primary school is a r_____ of passage.
15. Careful or the lion will b_____.
16. He used matches to ign_____ the fire.
17. The monkeys were quite a s_____.
18. It was a shock, but they will be alr_____.

74. Plurals – f and v

Words ending in 'ff' or 've' – just add as 's.'

Words ending in 'f' or 'fe' change the 'f' to a 'v' and add 'es.'

There are exceptions such as roof.

Write the plural of the words below:

cliff	_____	wave	_____
sieve	_____	curve	_____
loaf	_____	belief	_____
shelf	_____	leaf	_____
calf	_____	knife	_____
thief	_____	giraffe	_____
half	_____	wolf	_____
self	_____	hoof	_____
life	_____	chief	_____
scarf	_____	dwarf	_____

75. Homophones

Choose the correct word from the word bank:

> Word bank:
> summary, summery, dough, doe, doh, berth, birth, cheep, cheap, altar, alter, plum, plumb, naval, navel, chord, cord, wail, whale

1. To change. _____
   Part of a church or place of worship. _____
2. Where umbilical cord detached _____
   Related to the navy. _____
3. Sound of a young bird. _____
   Not expensive. _____
4. Test to determine the vertical. _____
   A type of fruit. _____
5. A high pitched cry of pain or grief. _____
   A marine mammal. _____
6. String or rope. _____
   Several musical notes played together _____
7. A bunk on a ship or train. _____
   To be born. _____
8. Warm, dry weather. _____
   A brief statement of the main points. _____
9. Mixture to make bread or pastry _____
   A female deer. _____
   The first note of a major scale. _____

76. Difficult spellings

One word in each sentence below is misspelled.
Underline the word and write it out correctly.

1. The book had come into her possesion
   some time previously. _____
2. He always prefered berry to
   chocolate ice-cream. _____
3. Please recieve this token of my
   appreciation. _____
4. Truely, it was an accident. _____
5. Due to unforseen circumstances,
   it was unavoidable. _____
6. I don't mind whereever we go. _____
7. Unfortunatly, she became very ill. _____
8. The stain was very noticable. _____
9. Is it really neccessary? _____
10. His knowlege of aircraft was
    excellent. _____

77. Synonyms

Choose the synonym of the words below:

Word bank:

infant, vital, possess, remote, kin, moveable, eternal, fascinate, pensive, drag, wary, region

	Synonym
mobile	
area	
distant	
relative	
thoughtful	
baby	
important	
everlasting	
intrigue	
own	
pull	
cautious	

78. Antonyms

Choose the antonym of the words below:

> Word bank:
> fabricated, concern, careless, assent, help, vacant, alert, create, reward, confess, forbid, graceful

	Antonym
disagree	
destroy	
punish	
occupied	
deny	
awkward	
true	
thwart	
weary	
apathy	
considerate	
allow	

79. Becoming a verb

Some suffixes change nouns or adjectives into verbs.

Add one of the suffixes: ate, en, ify or ise to the following words:

Word	Verb
acid	*acidify*
advert	
apology	
beauty	
class	
deep	
elastic	
identity	
length	
medicine	
memory	
person	
pollen	
simple	
standard	
active	

80. To be or not to be

Many verbs in English are irregular, that is they don't follow the standard pattern. One such verb, is the verb "to be."

	Present	Past
I	am	was
you	are	were
he / she / it	is	was
we	are	were
they	are	were

Write the correct form of the verb "to be" in the sentences below:

1. Yesterday, he _____ very late for work.
2. It _____ raining heavily, today.
3. We _____ going to come but she became ill.
4. You _____ correct, it _____ next Tuesday.
5. The puppy _____ playing happily, now.
6. I _____ very hungry, is lunch ready?
7. They _____ already very organised and the door's aren't due to open for two hours.
8. The Sports' Day _____ well run, last week.

81. Outer space

Put these in order from the smallest to the largest:

solar system, universe, galaxy, planet

_____, _____, _____, _____

Fill in the sentences below.

> Word bank
> star, day, rotates, orbits, moon, year, gas

The Earth _____ the sun, once every _____.

The _____ orbits the Earth.

The Earth _____ on its axis every _____.

The sun is a _____, which is a big ball of _____.

82. Homophones

Underline the correct word in the sentences below:

1. He (wood, **would**) have liked to go for a walk in the (**wood**, would) during Spring.
2. How he did (**moan**, mown) about how she had (moan, **mown**) the lawn.
3. He had to wait for his (heal, **heel**) to (**heal**, heel) before he could run again.
4. He wrote an (**ode**, owed) to his cat. She (ode, **owed**) her friend a meal.
5. They went for a walk and climbed over the (**stile**, style). The (stile, **style**) was very flamboyant.
6. The bird (**soared**, sword) overhead, while she flashed her (soared, **sword**) in the sunlight.
7. The (pole, **poll**) showed that most people were against erecting a (**pole**, poll) in the park.
8. The (bow, **bough**) of the tree was about to break. He would always (**bow**, bough) politely in greeting.
9. She (died, **dyed**) her hair, to cover the grey.
10. After falling in the (creak, **creek**), the chair tended to (**creak**, creek) when sat on.

83. Homographs

Which word has both of the meanings below?

> Word bank:
> organ, scale, bore, watch, fence, loom, sole, mine, novel, sentence, watch

1. The equipment used for making fabric by waving.
   Appear as a vague, threatening form. _____
2. New or unusual.
   Fiction story of book length. _____
3. Climb up or over something high.
   A series of musical notes. _____
4. A group of words that makes sense.
   Punishment for a crime. _____
5. Something that is dull and uninteresting.
   To make a hole in something. _____
6. The bottom of the foot.
   A type of flatfish. _____
7. A barrier.
   To participate in a sport that uses swords. _____
8. An excavation of the earth to extract minerals.
   Belonging to me. _____
9. To look.
   Used to tell the time. _____
10. A part of the body that has a particular function.
    An instrument that makes sound by air moving through pipes. _____

84. Plurals

Write the plural of the following words:

1. that　　　　　_____
2. child　　　　_____
3. axis　　　　　_____
4. louse　　　　_____
5. ox　　　　　　_____
6. goose　　　　_____
7. half　　　　　_____
8. index　　　　_____
9. sheep　　　　_____
10. antenna　　_____
11. fungus　　　_____
12. crisis　　　_____
13. series　　　_____
14. quiz　　　　_____
15. mouse　　　_____

Write the singular for the following words:

16. bacteria　　_____
17. dice　　　　_____
18. media　　　_____
19. formulae　_____
20. hooves　　_____

85. Idioms

Match the saying with the meaning:

Sayings:
1. Hit the nail on the head.
2. Hit the books.
3. Lend me your ears.
4. Rule of thumb.
5. Until the cows come home.
6. Penny for your thoughts.

Meanings:
A. Listen.
B. A long time.
C. Study.
D. Exactly right.
E. A rough estimate.
F. What are you thinking about?

Answers:
1. ____, 2. ____, 3. ____, 4. ____, 5. ____, 6. ____,

86. Antonyms

Choose the antonym of the words below:

> Word bank:
>
> calm, advance, dubious, manual, curtail, divulge, regard, rural, unique, dull, float, chaotic

	Antonym
hinder	
extend	
certain	
conceal	
automatic	
neglect	
tranquillity	
urban	
enrage	
submerge	
familiar	
vivid	

87. Comparatives and superlatives

Comparatives are used to compare two things. Superlatives are used to state which one is the most of something. Comparatives are generally formed by adding the suffix 'er,' while superlatives are formed by adding the suffix 'est.'

However, there are many exceptions. You may have heard the poem:
　Good, better best, never let it rest,
　　Until the good is better and the better is best.

Write the comparative and superlative for the words below:

Word	Comparative	Superlative
short	*shorter*	*shortest*
tall		
sad		
happy		
tidy		
good		
bad		
little		
much		

88. Difficult spellings

One word in each sentence below is misspelled. Underline the word and write it out correctly:

1. The flowers were luvly. _____
2. She was very nervus before the music exam. _____
3. The que for the canteen was long. _____
4. The preperation for the 11 plus exam took a lot of time. _____
5. He was disapointed with losing the tennis match. _____
6. The audiance applauded loudly. _____
7. The conclusen from the experiment was surprising. _____
8. It was hard to remove the permenant pen from the white board. _____
9. He did reserch on the benefits of a healthy diet. _____
10. They had one dorhter and two sons. _____

89. Collective nouns (not animals)

Match the collective noun with the objects:

> Word bank:
> constellation, battery, ream, choir, bank, anthology, peal, fleet, hug, range, collection, quiver, crowd, class, band, bouquet

Animal	Collective noun
angels	
arrows	
bells	
cars	
flowers	
monitors	
mountains	
musicians	
paper	
people	
poems	
stamps	
stars	
students	
teddy bears	
tests	

90. Idioms

Match the saying with the meaning:

Sayings:
1. Rome was not built in a day.
2. When pigs fly.
3. Run out of steam.
4. Sick as a dog.
5. Let the cat out of the bag.
6. To be under the weather.

Meanings:
A. Very sick
B. Have no energy.
C. Will never happen.
D. It will take time.
E. Feeling unwell.
F. Let a secret out.

Answers:
1. _____, 2. _____, 3. _____, 4. _____, 5. _____, 6. _____,

91. Shopping

Which shop would you buy the following, or get these services?

> Word bank:
>
> butcher, bakery, newsagent, pharmacy, greengrocer, deli (delicatessen), book shop, jeweller, charity shop, barber, florist, laundrette,

	shop
magazine	
fruit	
second hand clothing	
meat	
cheese	
flowers	
necklace	
bread	
book	
medicine	
male hair cut	
wash clothes	

92. Capital cities - Europe

Write the capital city for the following countries:

Country	Capital City
England	_____
Scotland	_____
Eire (Ireland)	_____
Northern Ireland	_____
France	_____
Germany	_____
Spain	_____
Italy	_____
Poland	_____
Sweden	_____
Denmark	_____
Netherlands	_____
Greece	_____
Hungary	_____
Finland	_____
Austria	_____
Czech Republic	_____
Ukraine	_____

93. In the garden

Match the garden terms to their definitions:

> Word bank:
>
> seed, trug, compost, fertiliser, rake, hoe, secateurs, spade, trowel

1. A long handled gardening tool with a thin metal blade. _____
2. A long handled gardening tool with a toothed end. _____
3. Garden tool with a sharp edged blade used for digging. _____
4. A pair of pruning clippers that can be used with one hand. _____
5. A shallow basket used for carrying garden produce. _____
6. A small hand held tool with a curved scoop. _____
7. When planted can grow into a plant. _____
8. Substance added to soil to enable plants to grow better. _____
9. Decayed plant or animal matter used as fertiliser. _____

94. Idioms

Match the saying with the meaning:

Sayings:
1. The straw that breaks the camel's back.
2. Know the ropes.
3. You can't judge a book by its cover.
4. To take with a pinch of salt.
5. Nest egg.
6. No room to swing a cat.

Meanings:
A. A small space.
B. A small issue or problem that makes everything else seem unbearable.
C. Do not completely believe it.
D. Understand the process used, how to do something.
E. Savings set aside for the future.
F. Quality or worth cannot be determined by the appearance.

Answers:
1. _____, 2._____, 3._____, 4._____, 5._____, 6._____,

95. Synonyms

Choose the synonym of the words below:

> Word bank:
>
> exile, adore, permit, kind, thermal, solemn, liberty, squalid, look, glisten, adhesive, neutral

	Synonym
cherish	_____
allow	_____
filthy	_____
impartial	_____
heat	_____
freedom	_____
banish	_____
serious	_____
peruse	_____
glue	_____
species	_____
sparkle	_____

96. Antonyms

Choose the antonym of the words below:

Word bank:

vague, fierce, lenient, loyalty, stubborn, peculiar, insolent, nimble, active, delighted, plain, improve,

	Antonym
ordinary	
courteous	
ornate	
compliant	
treachery	
passive	
deteriorate	
strict	
timid	
clumsy	
appalled	
precise	

97. Capital cities – non-European

Write the capital city for the following countries.

Country	Capital City
Japan	
China	
Australia	
New Zealand	
India	
Pakistan	
Indonesia	
Canada	
America (USA)	
Malaysia	
Brazil	
Egypt	
Kenya	
Tanzania	
Ethiopia	
Turkey	
Israel	
South Korea	

98. Homophones

Choose the correct word from the word bank:

> Word bank:
>
> leech, leach, lynx, links, dual, duel, wait, weight, weekly, weakly, buoy, boy, pare, pear, trussed, trust,

1. Using little strength. _____
2. Every seven days. _____
3. An anchored float. _____
4. A young male. _____
5. A type of wild cat. _____
6. Rings or loops in a chain. _____
7. To have tied up the legs of a chicken before cooking. _____
8. Belief in the reliability or ability of someone or something. _____
9. A type of worm, many are parasites. _____
10. Drain away from soil. _____
11. A contest between two parties. _____
12. Consisting of two parts. _____
13. Stay where one is, leave until later. _____
14. How heavy something is. _____
15. Cut away the outer edges. _____
16. A type of fruit. _____

99. Homographs

Which word has both of the meanings below?

> Word bank:
> bluff, squash, soil, firm, prune, bank, match, mole, fast, lap

1. A contest or series of games.
   A thing or person that resembles or corresponds to another. _____
2. A small, dark, raised blemish on the skin.
   Someone in an organisation that anonymously betrays confidential information. _____
3. To try to deceive someone that you are able to do something.
   A steep cliff. _____
4. Firmly attached.
   Moving quickly. _____
5. Solid and stable.
   A business. _____
6. The land beside a river or lake.
   A financial establishment. _____
7. A dried plum.
   To trim plants. _____
8. The flat area between the knees and waist when seated.
   One circuit of a track during a race. _____
9. A type of drink like a cordial.
   Crush with force so it becomes flat. _____
10. To make dirty.
    What plants grow in. _____

100. Onomatopoeia

Words that sound just like their meaning,
Words like splatter, boom and whining.
It's the hush and shoosh of a mumble,
Or the bang, clang, crash of a rumble.
It's the hissing, buzzing, quacks and chirps,
Before the argh, ou, ouch, oh no it hurts.
It's the bark, woof, miaow, go on shoo,
Before the atishoo, achoo, I need a tissue.
From the flitter, flutter of a butterfly,
To the vroom, zoom, zing of a plane up high.
Oodles and oodles of expression I see,
I think I should stop before you flee.

From the poem above, give an onomatopoeic word that means

1. Speak unclearly. _____
2. The noise of a snake. _____
3. The sound of a bird (not a duck) _____
4. A fight _____
5. Splash with a liquid. _____

Answers

1. Big and small

Small	Medium	Big
tiny	average	large
microscopic	medium	huge
infinitesimal	intermediate	enormous
miniature	moderate	colossal
minute		gargantuan
little		gigantic
miniscule		mammoth
small		massive
		monstrous
		humongous

2. Male and female relationships

Male	Female
brother	sister
nephew	niece
father	mother
uncle	aunt
husband	wife
grandfather	grandmother
son	daughter

3. Animal babies

Animal	Baby
cat	kitten
cow	calf
deer	fawn
dog	puppy
dolphin	pup
elephant	calf
giraffe	calf
goat	kid
horse	foal
lion	cub
pig	piglet
rabbit	kitten
sheep	lamb
zebra	foal

4. Where we live

In order: hamlet, village, town, city, county, country, continent.

Definition of hamlet: A small settlement, generally one smaller than a village.

5. –ice and –ise

    1. practise
    2. practice
    3. advise
    4. advice
    5. advice, practice
    6. devise, device, practise

6. Feathers and fins

Birds	Fish
heron	sole
kiwi	cod
grebe	trout
teal	herring
grouse	salmon
quail	bass
petrel	carp
cormorant	whiting
bittern	flounder
ibis	perch
spoonbill	hake
kite	plaice
tit	bream
buzzard	eel
coot	mackerel
tern	guppy

7. Measuring

	Units	
mass	gram	
length	metre	
volume	1. litre	2. metre cubed
speed	1. mile per hour	2. kilometre per hour
time	1. second	2. minute
temperature	degree Celcius	

Another word for volume is <u>capacity</u>.

8. Synonyms, antonyms and homophones
correct, left, write
damage, fix, brake

9. Idioms
1F, 2A, 3B, 4D, 5E, 6C

10. To, too, two
to, two, to, too, to, too, two, too

11. Words with more than one meaning
    1. relish
    2. light
    3. summit
    4. confidence
    5. stick

12. Difficult spellings

    Across
    1. fourth
    5. acceptable
    8. ache
    9. cough
    10. height

    Down
    2. occasion
    3. separate
    4. cemetery
    6. bought
    7. enough

13. Fast and slow

Fast	Slow
speedily	meandering
quickly	slowly
swift	leisurely
promptly	sluggish
frantic	sedate
rapid	crawl
hastily	plodding
hurriedly	dawdling

14. 'i' before 'e' except after 'c'

    1. ei 2. ei 3. ei 4. ie 5. ie
    6. ie 7. ei 8. ei 9. ie 10. ei

15. One, two, three

1	2	3
one	two	three
once	twice	thrice
single	double	triple
first	second	third

1. bi, tri, uni
2. mono
3. bi
4. di, mono

16. We're, wear, where and ware

1.	wear	6.	where
2.	where	7.	ware
3.	ware	8.	we're
4.	we're	9.	where
5.	wear	10.	wear

17. Instrument families

String	Woodwind	Brass
violin	bassoon	cornet
viola	piccolo	trumpet
double bass	flute	trombone
cello	clarinet	French horn
guitar	recorder	tuba
sitar	saxophone	bugle
banjo	oboe	
harp		
lute		

18. Idioms
1E, 2A, 3D, 4F, 5B, 6C

19. Word endings
1. al 2. le 3. le 4. al 5. il 6. el 7. le 8. el 9. al

20. Strong and weak synonyms
    1. annoyed, angry, furious
    2. cool, cold, freezing
    3. good, great, excellent
    4. content, happy, ecstatic
    5. melancholy, sad, depressed
    6. awkward, hard, difficult
    7. small, tiny, miniscule
    8. alright, nice, enchanting
    9. cheap, affordable, expensive
    10. peckish, hungry, ravenous
    11. moist, soggy, saturated

21. Difficult spelling
1. embarrassed
2. fiery
3. foreign
4. existence
5. exceed
6. guarantee
7. harass
8. hierarchy
9. ignorance
10. gauge

22. Synonyms
(in order) clever, part, commence, tip, bias, frugal, always, damp, mimic, stubborn, amaze, chuckle.

23. Old and new

Old	New
ancient	modern
antique	recent
stale	present
previous	fresh
past	current
aged	contemporary

24. Idioms
1E, 2D, 3A, 4F, 5B, 6C

25. Male and female

Male	Female
King	Queen
duke	duchess
host	hostess
prince	princess
count	countess
steward	stewardess
heir	heiress
hero	heroine
actor	actress

26. Body parts
Internal organs – lung, liver, brain, stomach, intestine, heart, kidney, pancreas

Elbow is to arm as *knee* is to leg.
Ankle is to leg as *wrist* is to arm.

1. heart 2. kidney 3. knuckle 4. lung
5. ear 6. arm 7. intestine 8. brain.

27. Difficult spelling

1. bizarre
2. colleague
3. committee
4. definitely
5. dilemma
6. ecstasy
7. familiar
8. friend
9. humorous
10. immediately
11. forty
12. Gist

28. Antonyms

untidy, disobedient, unusually, impolite, illogical, inaction, nonsense, inflexible, illegal, inappropriate, impure, unavailable, incomplete, disagree

29. Homophones

1. piece
2. quite
3. bare
4. leek
5. meet
6. whole, hole
7. bored
8. weak, week
9. aloud, allowed
10. pour

30. Religions

Religion	Person	Place of Worship
Christianity	Christian	Church
Hinduism	Hindu	Temple
Islam	Muslim	Mosque
Judaism	Jew	Synagogue
Sikhism	Sikh	Gurdwara

31. Adding –ing and –ed

Word	Add -ed	Add -ing
talk	talked	talking
hunt	hunted	hunting
cry	cried	crying
bore	bored	boring
surprise	surprised	surprising
lie	lied	lying
study	studied	studying
ski	skied	skiing
plan	planned	planning
exit	exited	exiting
answer	answered	answering
cancel	cancelled	cancelling
group	grouped	grouping
repair	repaired	repairing
bar	barred	barring
occur	occurred	occurring
stir	stirred	stirring
pour	poured	pouring
admit	admitted	admitting
target	targeted	targeting
traffic	trafficked	trafficking

32. Meat

Animal	Meat
young cow	veal
older cow	beef
deer	venison
pig	pork
pig (preserved)	bacon / ham
young sheep	lamb
older sheep	mutton

33. Idioms

1E, 2D, 3C, 4F, 5B, 6A

34. Difficult spelling

1. completely
2. conscious
3. curiosity
4. disappear
5. familiar
6. happened
7. independent
8. interrupt
9. knowledge
10. necessary
11. noticeable
12. occurrence
13. separate
14. surprise
15. truly

35. Synonyms

	Synonym
concur	agree
concise	brief
coax	persuade
honour	respect
sudden	abrupt
immature	juvenile
pacify	calm
hinder	impede
humiliate	shame
upright	erect
ludicrous	absurd
support	endorse

36. Antonyms

	Antonym
conventional	eccentric
chaos	order
artificial	natural
optimist	pessimist
serious	flippant
oblivious	aware
meagre	plentiful
tense	calm
captivity	wild
expand	contract
obvious	hidden
trivial	grave

37. Trees and flowers

Trees – beech, elm, larch, oak, conifer, yew, pine, mahogany, willow, poplar, hazel, maple, birch

Flowers – daffodil, lily, daisy, petunia, pansy, fuchsia, carnation, tulip, rhododendron, violet, buttercup, bluebell, geranium, cornflower, hyacinth, iris, orchid, honeysuckle, primrose

38. Words ending in -ance or –ence

absent	absence
allow	allowance
annoy	annoyance
appear	appearance
coherent	coherence
confident	confidence
conscious	conscience
different	difference
diligent	diligence
elegant	elegance
grieve	grievance
guide	guidance
ignore	ignorance
instant	instance
patient	patience
persist	persistence
relevant	relevance
resist	resistance

39. Idioms

1A, 2C, 3E, 4B, 5F, 6D

40. Homophones

1. hair 2. hare 3. tale 4. tail 5. serial 6. cereal 7. blue, 8. blew 9. sum, 10. some 11. vane 12. vein 13. vain

41. 'Shun' suffixes

Root word	Word with suffix added
act	*action*
complete	completion
confuse	confusion
connect	connection
demonstrate	demonstration
devote	devotion
direct	direction
distribute	distribution
electric	electrician
emit	emission
extend	extension
optic	optician
permit	permission
persuade	persuasion
possess	possession
promote	promotion
provide	provision
reduce	reduction
replicate	replication
success	succession

42. Synonyms

	Synonym
fall	tumble
blunt	curt
agree	consent
gluttonous	greedy
cultivate	grow
ruin	spoil
culprit	offender
gloomy	dismal
dirty	soil
shovel	scoop
lavish	excessive

| estimate | guess |

43. Antonyms

	Antonym
humble	arrogant
cautious	reckless
alert	lethargic
easy	cumbersome
robust	fragile
corrupt	virtuous
still	turbulent
feigned	real
recall	forget
neat	dishevelled
preceding	after
strengthen	debilitate

44. it's, its and who's, whose

1. Who's 2. Whose 3. It's 4. it's 5. its
6. Whose 7. Who's 8. It's 9. its 10. It's

45. Countries – Asia and South America

Asia	South America
Japan	Mexico
China	Peru
Malaysia	Argentina
Singapore	Brazil
India	Colombia
Pakistan	Ecuador
Thailand	Chile
Cambodia	Bolivia
Korea	Guyana
Mongolia	Paraguay
Brunei	Venezuela
Myanmar	Uruguay
Laos	
Nepal	
Vietnam	

46. Homographs
1. wind 2. well 3. coordinates 4. invalid 5. fan
6. lean 7. present 8. minute 9. chest 10. date

47 Difficult spelling
1. accommodate
2. foreseeable
3. glamorous
4. ancient
5. rhythm
6. sieve
7. supersede
8. accidentally
9. occurrence
10. height
11. acquire
12. column
13. library
14. maintenance
15. miniature
16. memento
17. government
18. happened
19. independent
20. interrupt

48. Plurals – words ending in 'o' and 'y'
1. solos
2. zoos
3. tomatoes
4. heroes
5. radios
6. logos
7. echoes
8. buffaloes (or buffalo)
9. mosquitoes
10. zeros
11. mangoes
12. tacos
13. libraries
14. berries
15. activities

49. Idioms
1C, 2A, 3F, 4E, 5B, 6D

50. Synonyms

	Synonym
proceed	continue
supple	flexible
miserly	stingy
solution	answer
impromptu	spontaneous
keen	eager
withdraw	retreat
assured	confident
secure	safe
regret	remorse
generous	bountiful
impartial	neutral

51. Antonyms

	antonym
recognise	ignore
hostile	friendly
important	trivial
real	fake
accomplish	fail
miserly	generous
rare	common
frivolous	serious
opaque	clear
scarce	ample
recede	advance
inept	competent

52. Homophones

1. guessed, guest 2. wore, war 3. boarder, border
4. receipt, reseat 5. maid, made 6. whet, wet 7. threw, through 8. mite, might 9. seize, seas 10. pier, peer

53. Countries – Europe and Africa

Europe	Africa
France	Tanzania
Belgium	Botswana
Spain	Tunisia
Hungary	Ghana
Turkey	Chad
Greece	Kenya
Ireland	Swaziland
Austria	Zimbabwe
Poland	Nigeria
Lichtenstein	Cameroon
Ukraine	Guinea
Germany	DR Congo
Denmark	Madagascar
England	

54. Difficult spelling

1. intelligent
2. graffiti
3. fierce
4. papyrus
5. deciduous
6. until
7. twelfth
8. schedule
9. publicly
10. questionnaire
11. pronunciation
12. pastime

55. Homographs

1. foot
2. swallow
3. close
4. band
5. bow
6. duck
7. refuse
8. pupil
9. bat
10. down

56. Idioms

1D, 2C, 3A, 4B, 5F, 6E

57. Colours

Red	Purple	Yellow / Orange	Blue / Green
cerise	violet	lemon	blue
burgundy	mauve	peach	aqua
rouge	purple	apricot	cyan
crimson	indigo	amber	azure
scarlet		cream	turquoise
maroon		gold	

58. Synonyms

	Synonym
unspoilt	pristine
bug	glitch
apply	implement
dominate	prevail
effect	consequence
passion	ardour
dependable	reliable
handle	manage
avid	zealous
opening	aperture
correct	amend
hint	suggestion

59. Antonyms

	Antonym
grave	merry
discover	hide
complicated	simple
pious	wicked
praise	jeer
meagre	ample
exposed	hidden
triumph	lose
odious	pleasant
futile	useful
pertinent,	unrelated
freeze	thaw

60. Sport

Team sports – volleyball, softball, lacrosse, hockey, football, netball, rounders, basketball

Board games – scrabble, chess, backgammon

1. bridge
2. badminton
3. dressage
4. diving
5. scrabble
6. chess
7. cycling
8. triathlon

61. There, they're and their
1. there
2. they're
3. their
4. they're
5. there
6. their
7. there
8. They're
9. their
10. they're

62. Homophones
1. ore, oars
2. time, thyme
3. humerus, humorous
4. urn, earn
5. route, root
6. steal, steel
7. sore, soar
8. heard, herd
9. currants, current
10. vial, vile

63. Homographs.
1. rock
2. clear
3. evening
4. ball
5. gum
6. sink
7. fine
8. incense
9. base
10. colon

64. Idioms
1E, 2C, 3A, 4F, 5D, 6B

65. Difficult spelling
1. licence
2. existence
3. eerie
4. extension
5. across
6. acrylic
7. abundant
8. loathe
9. maintain
10. obey
11. proceed
12. relevant

66. Collective nouns

Animal	Collective noun
ant	army (colony)
bat	colony
bee / wasp	swarm
bird	flock
buffalo	herd
butterfly	flutter
camel	caravan
crow	murder
dog	pack
dolphin	pod
fish	school (shoal)
giraffe	tower (herd)
lion	pride
owl	parliament
sheep	flock
squirrel	dray (colony)

67. Synonyms

	Synonym
spontaneous	impromptu
unstable	precarious
disappear	vanish
abandon	forsake
approach	method
detest	abhor
detestable	abominable
weak	feeble
admit	acknowledge
obvious	conspicuous
decay	decompose
harmful	detrimental

68. Antonyms

	Antonym
abundant	scarce
hasten	dawdle
industrious	lazy
economise	waste
accept	refuse
host	guest
landlord	tenant
ebb	flow
conceal	reveal
ignorance	knowledge
dawn	dusk
compulsory	voluntary

69. Prefixes

1. af (affix)
2. anti (antifreeze)
3. ad (adjective)
4. ad (advent)
5. ante (anteroom)
6. af (affluent)
7. pre (premature)
8. a (ablaze)
9. pre (predate)
10. out (outstanding)
11. ad (advise)
12. extra (extracurricular)
13. inter (international)
14. post (postpone)
15. over (overcast)
16. in (influx)
17. pre (prevent)
18. under (underarm)
19. semi (semiconscious)
20. pro (proactive)

70. Homographs
1. leaves
2. shed
3. park
4. lead
5. row
6. can
7. present
8. produce
9. desert
10. patient

71. Idioms
1A, 2E, 3B, 4F, 5C, 6D

72 Friends and foe

Friends	Foe
friend	foe
companion	enemy
ally	opponent
supporter	rival
comrade	adversary
associate	competitor
mate	combatant

73. –ight and –ite
1. ight (bright)
2. ite (kite)
3. ight (flight)
4. ite (write)
5. ite (excite)
6. ight (plight)
7. ite (polite)
8. ight (tight)
9. ight (night)
10. ight (right)
11. ite (white)
12. ight (might)
13. ite (mite)
14. ite (rite)
15. ite (bite)
16. ite (ignite)
17. ight (sight)
18. ight (alright)

74. Plurals – f and v

cliffs	waves
sieves	curves
loaves	beliefs
shelves	leaves
calves	knives
thieves	giraffes
halves	wolves
selves	hooves
lives	chiefs
scarves	dwarves

75. Homophones

1. alter, altar
2. navel, naval
3. cheep, cheap
4. plumb, plum
5. wail, whale
6. cord, chord
7. berth, birth
8. summery, summary
9. dough, doe, doh

76. Difficult spelling

1. possession
2. preferred
3. receive
4. truly
5. unforeseen
6. wherever
7. unfortunately
8. noticeable
9. necessary
10. knowledge

77. Synonyms

	Synonym
mobile	moveable
area	region
distant	remote
relative	kin
thoughtful	pensive
baby	infant
important	vital
everlasting	eternal
intrigue	fascinate
own	possess
pull	drag
cautious	wary

78. Antonyms

	Antonym
disagree	assent
destroy	create
punish	reward
occupied	vacant
deny	confess
awkward	graceful
true	fabricated
thwart	help
weary	alert
apathy	concern
considerate	careless
allow	forbid

79. Becoming a verb

Word	
acid	*acidify*
advert	advertise
apology	apologise
beauty	beautify
class	classify
deep	deepen
elastic	elasticise
identity	identify
length	lengthen
medicine	medicate
memory	memorise
person	personify or personalise
pollen	pollinate
simple	simplify
standard	standardise
active	activate

80. To be or not to be.

1. was
2. is
3. were
4. are, is
5. is
6. am
7. are
8. was

81. Outer Space
planet, solar system, galaxy, universe

orbits, year, moon, rotates, day, star, gas

82. Homophones

1. would, wood
2. moan, mown
3. heel, heal
4. ode, owed
5. stile, style
6. soared, sword
7. poll, pole
8. bough, bow
9. dyed
10. creek, creak

83. Homographs
1. loom
2. novel
3. scale
4. sentence
5. bore
6. sole
7. fence
8. mine
9. watch
10. organ

84. Plurals
1. those
2. children
3. axes
4. lice
5. oxen
6. geese
7. halves
8. indices
9. sheep
10. antennae
11. fungi
12. crises
13. series
14. quizzes
15. mice
16. bacterium
17. die
18. medium
19. formula
20. hoof

85. Idioms
1D, 2C, 3A, 4E, 5B, 6F

86 Antonyms

	Antonym
hinder	advance
extend	curtail
certain	dubious
conceal	divulge
automatic	manual
neglect	regard
tranquillity	chaotic
urban	rural
enrage	calm
submerge	float
familiar	unique
vivid	dull

87. Comparatives and superlatives

Word	Comparative	Superlative
short	*shorter*	*shortest*
tall	taller	tallest
sad	sadder	saddest
happy	happier	happiest
tidy	tidier	tidiest
good	better	best
bad	worse	worst
little	less	least
much	more	most

88. Difficult spelling

1. lovely
2. nervous
3. queue
4. preparation
5. disappointed
6. audience
7. conclusion
8. permanent
9. research
10. daughter

89. Collective nouns (not animals)

Animal	Collective noun
angels	choir
arrows	quiver
bells	peal
cars	fleet
flowers	bouquet
monitors	bank
mountains	range
musicians	band
paper	ream
people	crowd
poems	anthology
stamps	collection
stars	constellation
students	class
teddy bears	hug
tests	battery

90. Idioms

1D, 2C, 3B, 4A, 5F, 6E

91. Shopping

	shop
magazine	newsagent
fruit	greengrocer
second hand clothing	charity shop
meat	butcher
cheese	deli
flowers	florist
necklace	jeweller
bread	bakery
book	book shop
medicine	pharmacy
male hair cut	barber
wash clothes	laundrette

92. Capital Cities – Europe

Coungtry	Capital City
England	London
Scotland	Edinburgh
Eire (Ireland)	Dublin
Northern Ireland	Belfast
France	Paris
Germany	Berlin
Spain	Madrid
Italy	Rome (Roma)
Poland	Warsaw (Warszawa)
Sweden	Stockholm
Denmark	Copenhagen (København)
Netherlands	Amsterdam
Greece	Athens
Hungary	Budapest
Finland	Helsinki (Helsingfors)
Austria	Vienna (Wien)
Czech Republic	Prague (Praha)
Ukraine	Kiev (Kyïv)

93. In the garden

1. hoe
2. rake
3. spade
4. secateurs
5. trug
6. trowel
7. seed
8. fertiliser
9. compost

94. Idioms

1B, 2D, 3F, 4C, 5E, 6A

95. Synonyms

	Synonym
cherish	adore
allow	permit
filthy	squalid
impartial	neutral
heat	thermal
freedom	liberty
banish	exile
serious	solemn
peruse	look
glue	adhesive
species	kind
sparkle	glisten

96. Antonyms

	Antonym
ordinary	peculiar
courteous	insolent
ornate	plain
compliant	stubborn
treachery	loyalty
passive	active
deteriorate	improve
strict	lenient
timid	fierce
clumsy	nimble
appalled	delighted
precise	vague

97. Capital cities – non-European

Country	Capital City
Japan	Tokyo
China	Beijing
Australia	Canberra
New Zealand	Wellington
India	New Delhi
Pakistan	Islamabad
Indonesia	Jakarta
Canada	Ottawa
America (USA)	Washington DC
Malaysia	Kuala Lumpur
Brazil	Brasília
Egypt	Cairo
Kenya	Nairobi
Tanzania	Dodoma
Ethiopia	Addis Ababa
Turkey	Ankara
Israel	Jerusalem
South Korea	Seoul

98. Homophones

1. weakly
2. weekly
3. buoy
4. boy
5. lynx
6. links
7. trussed
8. trust
9. leech
10. leach
11. duel
12. dual
13. wait
14. weight
15. pare
16. pear

99. Homographs
1. match
2. mole
3. bluff
4. fast
5. firm
6. bank
7. prune
8. lap
9. squash
10. soil

100. Onomatopoeia
1. mumble
2. hissing
3. chirps
4. rumble
5. splatter

www.ingramcontent.com/pod-product-compliance
Lightning Source LLC
Chambersburg PA
CBHW071511040426
42444CB00008B/1595